GOLDA MEIR

GOLDA MEIR

Karen McAuley

1985
CHELSEA HOUSE PUBLISHERS
NEW YORK

MANAGING EDITOR: William P. Hansen
ASSOCIATE EDITOR: John Haney
CONSULTANT: Mark Sufrin
EDITORIAL STAFF: Jennifer Caldwell
                 Katherine Melchior
                 Susan Quist
ART DIRECTOR: Susan Lusk
LAYOUT: Irene Friedman
COVER DESIGN: Susan Lusk
PICTURE RESEARCH: Leah Malamed, John Haney

First Printing

Library of Congress Cataloging in Publication Data
McAuley, Karen.
Golda Meir.

(World leaders past & present)
Bibliography: p.
Includes index.
Summary: A biography of the American Jew who moved to
Palestine and dedicated her life to the creation and
preservation of a Jewish state.
1. Meir, Golda, 1898-1978—Juvenile literature.
2. Prime ministers—Israel—Biography—Juvenile literature.
[1. Meir, Golda, 1898-1978. 2. Prime ministers]
I. Title. II. Series.
DS126.6.M42M33 1985 956.94'053'0924 [B][92] 84-27475
ISBN 0-87754-568-5

Chelsea House Publishers
Harold Steinberg, Chairman & Publisher
Susan Lusk, Vice President
A Division of Chelsea House Educational Communications, Inc.

Chelsea House Publishers
133 Christopher Street
New York, N.Y. 10014

Photos courtesy of AP/Wide World Photos

Contents

C H E L S E A   H O U S E   P U B L I S H E R S

W O R L D   L E A D E R S   P A S T   &   P R E S E N T

Further titles in preparation

ON LEADERSHIP
Arthur M. Schlesinger, jr.

LEADERSHIP, it may be said, is really what makes the world go round. Love no doubt smooths the passage; but love is a private transaction between consenting adults. Leadership is a public transaction with history. The idea of leadership affirms the capacity of individuals to move, inspire and mobilize masses of people so that they act together in pursuit of an end. Sometimes leadership serves good purposes, sometimes bad; but whether the end is benign or evil, great leaders are those men and women who leave their personal stamp on history.

Now, the very concept of leadership implies the proposition that individuals can make a difference. This proposition has never been universally accepted. From classical times to the present day, eminent thinkers have regarded individuals as no more than the agents and pawns of larger forces, whether the gods and goddesses of the ancient world or, in the modern era, race, class, nation, the dialectic, the will of the people, the spirit of the times, history itself. Against such forces, the individual dwindles into insignificance.

So contends the thesis of historical determinism. Tolstoy's great novel *War and Peace* offers a famous statement of the case. Why, Tolstoy asked, did millions of men in the Napoleonic wars, denying their human feelings and their common sense, move back and forth across Europe slaughtering their fellows? "The war," Tolstoy answered, "was bound to happen simply because it was bound to happen." All prior history predetermined it. As for leaders, they, Tolstoy said, "are but the labels that serve to give a name to an end and, like labels, they have the least possible connection with the event." The greater the leader, "the more conspicuous the inevitability and the predestination of every act he commits." The leader, said Tolstoy, is "the slave of history."

Determinism takes many forms. Marxism is the determinism of class, Nazism the determinism of race. But the idea of men and women as the slaves of history runs athwart the deepest human instincts. Rigid determinism abolishes the idea of human freedom—the assumption of free choice that underlies every move we make, every word we speak, every thought we think. It abolishes the idea of human responsibility, since it is manifestly unfair to reward or punish people for actions that are by definition beyond their control. No one can live consistently by any deterministic creed. The Marxist states prove this themselves by their extreme susceptibility to the cult of leadership.

More than that, history refutes the idea that individuals make no difference. In December 1931 a British politician crossing Park Avenue in New York City between 76th and 77th Streets around ten-thirty at night looked in the wrong direction and was knocked down by an automobile—a moment, he later recalled, of a man aghast, a world aglare: "I do not understand why I was not broken like an eggshell or squashed like a gooseberry." Fourteen months later an American politician, sitting in an open car in Miami, Florida, was fired on by an assassin; the man beside him was hit. Those who believe that individuals make no difference to history might well ponder whether the next two decades would have been the same had Mario Contasini's car killed Winston Churchill in 1931 and Giuseppe Zangara's bullet killed Franklin Roosevelt in 1933. Suppose, in addition, that Adolf Hitler had been killed in the street fighting during the Munich *Putsch* of 1923 and that Lenin had died of typhus during the First World War. What would the 20th century be like now?

For better or for worse, individuals do make a difference. "The notion that a people can run itself and its affairs anonymously," wrote the philosopher William James, "is now well known to be the silliest of absurdities. Mankind does nothing save through initiatives on the part of inventors, great or small, and imitation by the rest of us—these are the sole factors in human progress. Individuals of genius show the way, and set the patterns, which common people then adopt and follow."

Leadership, James suggests, means leadership in thought as well as in action. In the long run, leaders in thought may well make the greater difference to the world. But, as Woodrow Wilson once said, "Those only are leaders of men, in the general eye, who lead in action. . . . It is at their hands that new thought gets its translation into the crude language of deeds." Leaders in thought often invent in solitude and obscurity, leaving to later generations the tasks of imitation. Leaders in action—the leaders portrayed in this series— have to be effective in their own time.

And they cannot be effective by themselves. They must act in response to the rhythms of their age. Their genius must be adapted, in a phrase of William James's, "to the receptivities of the moment." Leaders are useless without followers. "There goes the mob," said the French politician hearing a clamor in the streets. "I am their leader. I must follow them." Great leaders turn the inchoate emotions of the mob to purposes of their own. They seize on the opportunities of their time, the hopes, fears, frustrations, crises, potentialities.

8

They succeed when events have prepared the way for them, when the community is waiting to be aroused, when they can provide the clarifying and organizing ideas. Leadership ignites the circuit between the individual and the mass and thereby alters history.

It may alter history for better or for worse. Leaders have been responsible for the most extravagant follies and most monstrous crimes that have beset suffering humanity. They have also been vital in such gains as humanity has made in individual freedom, religious and racial tolerance, social justice and respect for human rights.

There is no sure way to tell in advance who is going to lead for good and who for evil. But a glance at the gallery of men and women in *World Leaders—Past and Present* suggests some useful tests.

One test is this: do leaders lead by force or by persuasion? By command or by consent? Through most of history leadership was exercised by the divine right of authority. The duty of followers was to defer and to obey. "Theirs not to reason why,/ Theirs but to do and die." On occasion, as with the so-called "enlightened despots" of the 18th century in Europe, absolutist leadership was animated by humane purposes. More often, absolutism nourished the passion for domination, land, gold and conquest and resulted in tyranny.

The great·revolution of modern times has been the revolution of equality. The idea that all people should be equal in their legal condition has undermined the old structures of authority, hierarchy and deference. The revolution of equality has had two contrary effects on the nature of leadership. For equality, as Alexis de Tocqueville pointed out in his great study *Democracy in America*, might mean equality in servitude as well as equality in freedom.

"I know of only two methods of establishing equality in the political world," Tocqueville wrote. "Rights must be given to every citizen, or none at all to anyone . . . save one, who is the master of all." There was no middle ground "between the sovereignty of all and the absolute power of one man." In his astonishing prediction of 20th-century totalitarian dictatorship, Tocqueville explained how the revolution of equality could lead to the "*Führerprinzip*" and more terrible absolutism than the world had ever known.

But when rights are given to every citizen and the sovereignty of all is established, the problem of leadership takes a new form, becomes more exacting than ever before. It is easy to issue commands and enforce them by the rope and the stake, the concentration camp and the *gulag*. It is much harder to use argument and achievement to overcome opposition and win consent. The Founding Fathers of the United States understood the difficulty. They believed that history had given them the opportunity to decide, as

Alexander Hamilton wrote in the first Federalist Paper, whether men are indeed capable of basing government on "reflection and choice, or whether they are forever destined to depend . . . on accident and force."

Government by reflection and choice called for a new style of leadership and a new quality of followership. It required leaders to be responsive to popular concerns, and it required followers to be active and informed participants in the process. Democracy does not eliminate emotion from politics; sometimes it fosters demagoguery; but it is confident that, as the greatest of democratic leaders put it, you cannot fool all of the people all of the time. It measures leadership by results and retires those who overreach or falter or fail.

It is true that in the long run despots are measured by results too. But they can postpone the day of judgment, sometimes indefinitely, and in the meantime they can do infinite harm. It is also true that democracy is no guarantee of virtue and intelligence in government, for the voice of the people is not necessarily the voice of God. But democracy, by assuring the rights of opposition, offers built-in resistance to the evils inherent in absolutism. As the theologian Reinhold Niebuhr summed it up, "Man's capacity for justice makes democracy possible, but man's inclination to injustice makes democracy necessary."

A second test for leadership is the end for which power is sought. When leaders have as their goal the supremacy of a master race or the promotion of totalitarian revolution or the acquisition and exploitation of colonies or the protection of greed and privilege or the preservation of personal power, it is likely that their leadership will do little to advance the cause of humanity. When their goal is the abolition of slavery, the liberation of women, the enlargement of opportunity for the poor and powerless, the extension of equal rights to racial minorities, the defense of the freedoms of expression and opposition, it is likely that their leadership will increase the sum of human liberty and welfare.

Leaders have done great harm to the world. They have also conferred great benefits. You will find both sorts in this series. Even "good" leaders must be regarded with a certain wariness. Leaders are not demigods; they put on their trousers one leg after another just like ordinary mortals. No leader is infallible, and every leader needs to be reminded of this at regular intervals. Irreverence irritates leaders but is their salvation. Unquestioning submission corrupts leaders and demeans followers. Making a cult of a leader is always a mistake. Fortunately hero worship generates its own antidote. "Every hero," said Emerson, "becomes a bore at last."

The signal benefit the great leaders confer is to embolden the rest of us to live according to our own best selves, to be active, insistent, and resolute in affirming our own sense of things. For great leaders attest to the reality of human freedom against the supposed inevitabilities of history. And they attest to the wisdom and power that may lie within the most unlikely of us, which is why Abraham Lincoln remains the supreme example of great leadership. A great leader, said Emerson, exhibits new possibilities to all humanity. "We feed on genius. . . . Great men exist that there may be greater men."

Great leaders, in short, justify themselves by emancipating and empowering their followers. So humanity struggles to master its destiny, remembering with Alexis de Tocqueville: "It is true that around every man a fatal circle is traced beyond which he cannot pass; but within the wide verge of that circle he is powerful and free; as it is with man, so with communities."

—*New York*

1

Creating a Jewish Homeland

At 4:00 P.M. on May 14, 1948, the ceremony to establish a Jewish state in the land of Israel began. David Ben-Gurion, a small man with a shining face and a mane of bushy gray hair, stood up and struck a gavel on a table. The crowd in the Tel Aviv Art Museum rose and spontaneously began to sing. Never had the "Hatikvah" been sung more joyfully! "Hatikvah" means "hope" in Hebrew. The song was to be the anthem of the new nation.

When the singing ended, Ben-Gurion cleared his throat and began to read the Scroll of Independence:

"The Land of Israel was the birthplace of the Jewish people. Here their spiritual, religious, and national identity was formed. Here they achieved independence and created a culture of national and universal significance. Here they wrote and gave the Bible to the world. Exiled from the Land of Israel the Jewish people remained faithful to it in all the centuries of their dispersion, never ceasing to pray and hope for their return and the restoration of their national freedom."

Ben-Gurion's voice filled with emotion as he

Golda Meyerson signs the official Scroll of Independence, May 14, 1948. Unable to find real scroll parchment anywhere in Tel Aviv, Otto Walisch, who later became head of Israel's advertising union, found and tested a convincing substitute onto which he later transcribed the text of the declaration.

National Council members attend the signing of Israel's declaration of independence in Tel Aviv, May 14, 1948. The National Council acted as Israel's provisional government until February 17, 1949, when an elected government took office. A portrait of Theodor Herzl, the 19th-century Austrian dramatist who founded modern Zionism, dominates the assembly.

13

David Ben-Gurion, Israel's first prime minister, stands with an aide who displays the official Scroll of Independence. The Israeli government kept the scroll in a bank vault for six weeks after the independence ceremonies, until a truce ended the first round of fighting in the 1948 Arab-Israeli War.

continued: "We, the members of the National Council, representing the Jewish people in the Land of Israel and the Zionist movement . . . do hereby proclaim the establishment of a Jewish state in the Land of Israel—the state of Israel."

Among the hundreds of people jammed into the hot, crowded hall was Golda Mabovitch Meyerson. Her face was calm and strong, her gray eyes brimmed with tears. Along with the other members of the National Council, she had worked hard to make this day a reality.

German soldiers escort Jews from the ghetto in Warsaw, Poland, in 1943. Many survivors of the German concentration camps, where 6 million Jews died during World War II, emigrated to Palestine after the war, often at great risk since the British mandatory government there exercised harsh controls, often using force against illegal immigrants.

At last we have done it, Golda thought. For the first time in almost 20 centuries we have a land of our own! And no matter what happens next, no matter how we must pay for it, Jews have a nation. We are no longer helpless!

By the time it was her turn to sign the proclamation, Golda was weeping openly—tears of grief and joy. She cried for the millions of Jews through-

AUSCHWITZ I
OSWIECI
25 AUG

COMMANDANT'S HOUSE

CAMP HQ

CAMP ADMIN

GAS CHAMBER AND CREMATORIUM I

The Nazi concentration camp at Auschwitz in Poland, photographed by an Allied reconnaissance aircraft in 1944. While the evidence reaching Allied leaders increased during World War II, the full extent of Nazi atrocities against the Jews only became apparent when Allied forces overran and liberated the camps in 1945.

16

out history who had been tortured, killed, and driven from one country to another, the millions who had never known any place they could live without fear. And she wept with joy for the strength and security that the existence of a Jewish homeland would give to her children and grandchildren. Just knowing it was there would change their lives. Oh, how their lives would be different from her own!

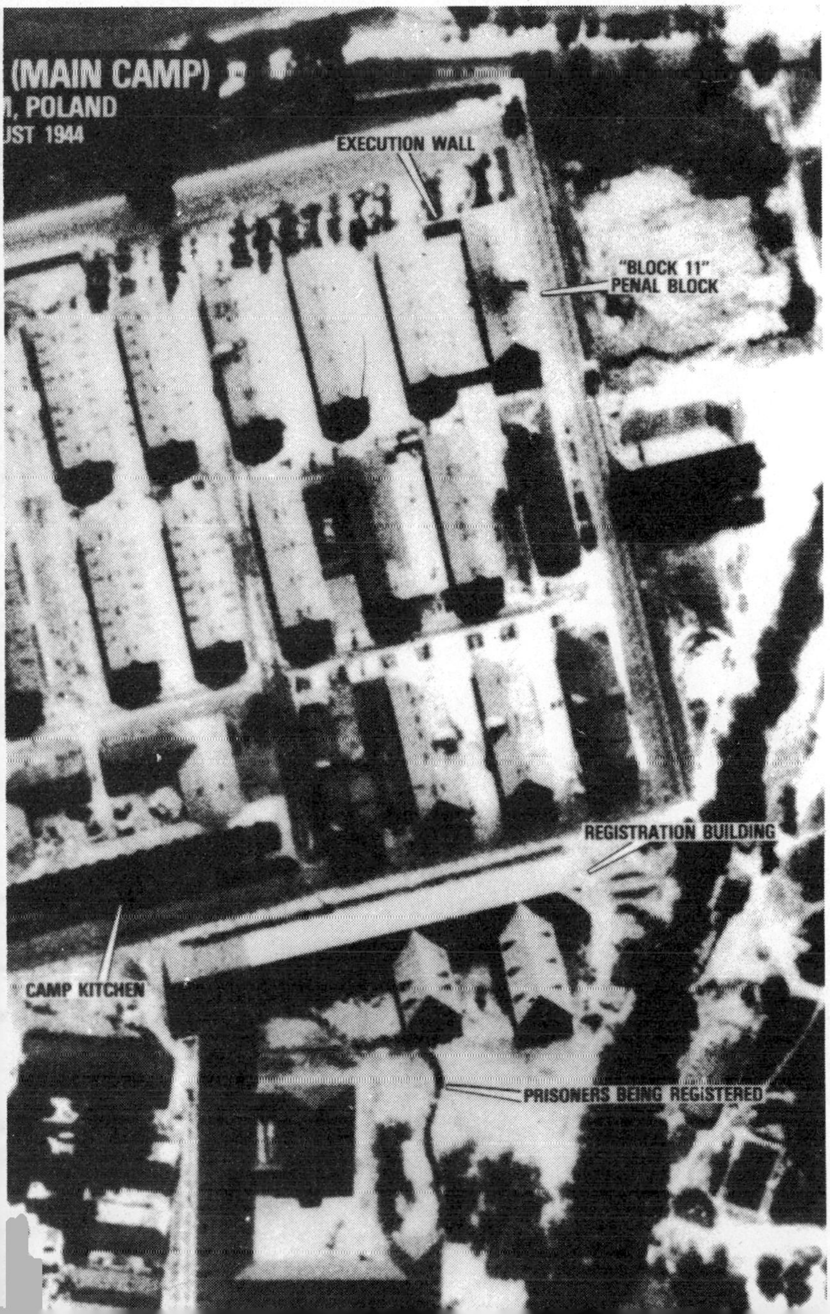

(MAIN CAMP)
, POLAND
UST 1944

EXECUTION WALL

"BLOCK 11"
PENAL BLOCK

REGISTRATION BUILDING

CAMP KITCHEN

PRISONERS BEING REGISTERED

Zionism, redemption, and rescue coalesced into one concept; if there are no Jews, there is no redemption; if there is to be redemption, a free Jewish people, Jews must first be rescued from death and destruction and brought to Palestine.
—GOLDA MEIR
in a speech to the
22nd Zionist Congress in 1946

2

Childhood in Russia

Golda was born and spent the first years of her life in Kiev, in the Russian Ukraine. Even as a little child, Golda learned something firsthand about the persecution of Jews. In 1902, at the age of four, she watched her father nail boards over the doors and windows of their home. When Golda asked him why he was doing that, he told her that an angry crowd of peasants, armed with sticks and knives, was heading toward town looking for Jews. Though she could not understand why anyone would want to hurt Jews, the little girl knew the danger was real. Her parents had told her about the widespread anti-Semitism in Russia.

Though a Jew-hating mob did not come that night, a year later in another part of Russia called Kishinev, 45 Jews were killed and more than a thousand homes and shops were looted or destroyed. People were maimed and tortured. Yet only once did the Russian police do anything, and that was to take clubs and sticks away from the Jews who were trying to defend themselves!

In protest Jewish communities everywhere decided to conduct a day-long fast. Five-year-old Golda wanted to join the protest. Though her grandfather told her she was much too young to go without food all day, she refused to listen to him. She ate nothing.

Russian peasants in Moscow, photographed in 1913 by the French artist Alphonse Mucha. The Russia of Golda's childhood was an agrarian, feudal state ruled by an autocratic monarch. Widespread poverty, allied with the complete lack of political representation, eventually led to a communist revolution in Russia in 1917.

A view of the Russian city of Kiev, Golda Meir's birthplace, shortly before German forces captured it in 1941. The Russians refer to Kiev, which was founded before the ninth century, as "the mother of cities."

In some ways Golda's family lived well, especially when compared to other Jews in Russia. Because her father was a skilled carpenter, the family was permitted to live beyond the pale, or outside of the sections set aside for Jews. Papa Mabovitch always had work, though he did have special problems as a Jew. Sometimes, when customers discovered that the cabinet-maker was a Jew, they refused to pay him. In Russia Jews were not allowed to use the courts to demand justice, so clients were not obligated to pay Jews for their work if they chose not to.

In 1903 it became clear to Golda's father that he could not live comfortably in Russia. Like thousands of others, he decided to try his luck in the United States. There a skilled worker would be paid for his labor, no matter what his religion. So the elder Mabovitch sold his carpentry tools and most of the family's belongings to buy passage on a steamship. After he had earned enough money to start a new home, he would send for his wife, Bluma, and their three daughters. In the meantime Bluma, Sheyna, who was then 14, Golda, and baby Tzipke went to live with Bluma's father in Pinsk.

At the time, revolutionary ideas were spreading throughout Russia and instilling hope in the oppressed. Many Jews longed for the day when the czar would be overthrown. Perhaps under a new government Jews would no longer be persecuted.

In Pinsk Sheyna soon became involved with a group of young political activists. They met secretly to discuss anti-Semitism and ways to combat it. When the meetings were held in Sheyna's house, little Golda listened intently. It was then that she first heard of the movement called Zionism that was to become so important to her.

Zionism is the movement to rebuild a Jewish state in Palestine. The movement started spontaneously in various parts of Europe toward the end of the 19th century. The separate elements of the movement came together when Theodor Herzl, an Austrian writer, convened the first Zionist Congress in 1897. From that time on, building a Jew-

ish Home in Palestine became an international movement.

Two thousand years earlier, Jews had lived and ruled themselves in Zion, or Eretz Israel as it is called in Hebrew. In 70 A.D. Roman conquerors drove them out and renamed the land Palestine. Though only a few Jewish families remained there, for centuries Palestine continued to be the longed-for home of Jews all over the world.

In the 1880s Jews from Eastern Europe began

Cossacks at an equestrian meeting in Moscow in 1937. The cossacks, who served as irregular cavalry for the czars for many years, often initiated anti-Semitic massacres, which explains the fear they inspired throughout Russia's Jewish communities.

moving back into Palestine, though they were not welcomed by the Ottoman Turks, Moslems who had ruled the region since the 16th century. Most of those immigrants were idealistic young scholars, craftsmen, and merchants fleeing persecution. They had neither the money nor the practical skills to rebuild the homeland. Yet, they were determined. Though many had to make a two-year journey on foot to reach Palestine, by 1914 their number had swelled to 115,000.

One of the leaders of the young Zionists in Pinsk was a quiet, gifted young mathematician, who had given up his studies to join the revolutionary movement. His name was Shamai Korngold. He visited the Mabovitch home often and soon fell in love with Sheyna. Golda listened excitedly to their whispered conversations about the growing number of revolutionaries in town and the regiments of cossacks (Russian soldiers) who were determined to cut them down.

Soviet army officers inspect the key to the Kiev fortress in 1944. Along with many other Russian cities, Kiev suffered terrible damage at the hands of the German invaders during World War II.

As Sheyna's involvement in radical politics heightened, Bluma Mabovitch began fearing for her family's safety. She wrote to her husband begging him to send money for them to come to America as soon as possible.

Finally, in 1905, a letter arrived from Milwaukee directing Bluma to make arrangements for the journey. The family had to obtain false identification, since Papa had previously helped a friend's wife and children to leave Russia by claiming they were his own.

The journey was long, arduous, and full of delays. Finally, after two days of restless waiting in an overcrowded immigration center, Bluma, Sheyna, Golda, and Tzipke boarded a ship for the 14-day journey to America.

A 1948 meeting of the Israeli government is dominated by a portrait of Theodor Herzl, the Austrian playwright and journalist who convened the First Zionist Congress in 1897. Herzl, a refined and educated man, stayed aloof from political and Jewish affairs until stung into an awareness of modern anti-Semitism, especially as it was manifested in France in the early 1890s, at the time of the Dreyfus trial.

3

Growing Up in Milwaukee

When the exhausted family finally reached Milwaukee, they were met by Papa at the railroad station. To Golda he seemed to have become a stranger. He had shaved off his beard and now dressed like an American. Getting used to him and the strange new world of Milwaukee would take time.

Golda spent her first few days in America in a trance. In her eyes Milwaukee was incredible. She later wrote, "Everything looked so colorful and fresh, as though it had just been created, and I stood for hours staring at the traffic and the people." Bicycles, cars, and trolleys flashed by! Watching them and all the other miracles of American life—like running water at the turn of a faucet, and electric lights—young Golda sometimes found herself wondering just who and where she was.

Papa was undoubtedly glad to see his wife and daughters. But they looked so dowdy and old-fashioned to him in their Russian clothes. The morning after they arrived, he marched his family downtown for a shopping expedition. His first purchases would be for Sheyna. Papa picked out a frilly blouse and a broad-brimmed straw hat covered with bright flowers.

Most important, I cannot remember any period when we thought only of our personal affairs. Our home was always involved in causes of some kind.
—GOLDA MEIR
speaking of her
childhood in Milwaukee

Golda Mabovitch at age eight, shortly after she arrived in the United States.

A view of Milwaukee, Wisconsin, in 1945. The building in the foreground is City Hall, which was formally opened in 1895. Many European immigrants, including Russian Jews, settled in Milwaukee during the late 19th and early 20th centuries, bringing with them a tradition of socialism still in evidence in the city's politics today.

"Now you look like a human being! This is how we dress in America," Papa said proudly. Sheyna was insulted by his efforts to transform her.

The conflict between Sheyna and her father was not the only tension in the Mabovitches' new household. Their first apartment on Walnut Street consisted of two rooms, a tiny closet-sized kitchen, and a long hallway that led to a small, dark, dirty store. Industrious Bluma saw its possibilities at once. Though she did not speak a word of English, and had never even worked in a shop before, she soon opened a grocery that sold milk, rolls, eggs, sugar, and a few other staples.

But Papa was deeply hurt. He felt that the little store showed Bluma's lack of faith in his ability to make a living for his family, and he would have no part of shopkeeping. Sheyna also refused to help out in the grocery. "I did not come to America to turn into a shopkeeper, a social parasite," she protested. Instead, Sheyna got a job in a factory where she could work among laborers. Though she often exasperated her parents, Sheyna insisted on living according to her own principles. Thus, on most mornings while Mother went to the market to purchase fresh supplies, the burden of opening the shop fell to nine-year-old Golda.

On many mornings Golda was late for school because of her work at the store. She hated this. As a little girl attending the Fourth Street School, near Milwaukee's famous Schlitz beer factory, Golda was an avid student. When she was late, she often ran to school crying all the way from frustration.

Apart from this, Golda enjoyed life in Milwaukee. School excited her, and she made many new friends. In fact, with so much to see and do, she was no longer haunted by her memories of fear and persecution in Pinsk.

This was not so for young Tzipke. Shortly after they arrived, Golda, Tzipke, and their mother attended a Labor Day parade. They stood on a street corner to watch for Papa, who was marching with the carpenters' union. At the first sight of the mounted police who were leading the marchers, Tzipke screamed, "It's the cossacks! The cossacks

are coming!"

Golda reacted very differently to the same scene. She was delighted by the contrast between life in America and Russia. That day in Milwaukee, mounted police were actually escorting the marchers instead of forcing them to disperse or trampling them underfoot as they did in Russia. Golda was keenly aware of what such freedom meant. She understood that by exercising her rights as an American, she could help to correct the problems she saw.

Though Golda was delighted by her life in Milwaukee, her 17-year-old sister was depressed by it. Sheyna had come to the United States against her will, leaving her revolutionary activities and her boyfriend, Shamai, behind. In Milwaukee she refused to work in the grocery store and complained about the difficulty of finding a suitable husband. Eventually, Sheyna left home and supported herself by working in clothing factories.

Sheyna's spirits lifted considerably when Shamai finally came to the United States and settled in Milwaukee. Though her parents objected strongly, the couple continued their courtship. Sheyna and Shamai adored each other. Together, Sheyna felt, they could overcome almost any obstacle. Shamai soon found work in a cigarette factory and the two of them studied English at night. However, Sheyna contracted tuberculosis and had to go to the Jewish Hospital for Consumptives in Denver, Colorado. Later, Shamai joined her and they were married.

Though the Mabovitches refused even to write to their defiant daughter, Golda kept in touch with her. To Golda, Sheyna was an inspiration. Years later, in her autobiography, she described her older sister as "a shining example, my dearest friend,

Golda Mabovitch (at right, in white dress) with classmates at Milwaukee's Fourth Street School in 1911. The mayor of Milwaukee presented Golda with a large framed print of the photograph when she visited the city during an American tour in 1969.

and my mentor." Golda's letters, written with increasing improvement in English, told of her progress at school, and of the family's continuing struggles. In one letter, Golda glowingly described her first public speaking appearance and fundraiser, calling it "the greatest success that there ever was in Packen Hall."

Although education was free in Milwaukee, students had to pay a small charge for textbooks. Golda realized that many children could not afford the fee. She decided to do something about this. She and her best friend, Regina Hamburger, organized a group of girls to raise money for school books. The American Young Sisters Society, as they called themselves, rented a hall and sent out invitations to a Saturday night "ball" featuring speeches, tea, and sandwiches. Dozens of people came.

The program was simple: Golda spoke and Tzipke recited a poem. Though her mother had begged her to write out her speech, Golda's instinct was just to stand up and say what was in her heart. The tall young girl, her heavy chestnut braids bobbing, spoke so earnestly that her audience contributed enough money to supply books for all the poor children in the Fourth Street School.

During her years in Milwaukee, Golda's education had become deeply important to her. She and Regina planned to enter high school together in 1912. But in those days, young people did not automatically go on to high school. Unless they were outstanding students or extremely ambitious, most poor children got working papers and began helping to support their families.

Golda's parents never took her desire for an education seriously. When Golda told them she wanted to go not only to high school but to college to train as a teacher, they objected strenuously. She ought to be more practical! Education was a luxury, they told her. Besides, education wasn't good for women. "It doesn't pay to be too clever," her father warned. "Men don't like smart girls!" It was time, they said, for Golda to think seriously about getting married. Why, where was her concern for her parents? A loyal daughter would be working full time in her family's grocery.

The same conflict in values that drove Sheyna away, now confronted Golda. She argued with her parents and cried, but without success. Yet, from far away in Denver, Shamai and Sheyna encouraged Golda to pursue her education. Golda's correspondence with them had increased, despite the fact that the couple could not write to Golda at home. Instead, their letters had to be sent to Regina Hamburger's house.

In the fall of 1912, Golda defiantly started her first term at North Division High School. After school and on weekends she worked at a variety of odd jobs so that she would not have to ask her parents for money. But the arguments at home continued. Finally, the break came when Bluma began to arrange a marriage for 14-year-old Golda with a man more than twice her age! Golda was furious. She wrote to Shamai and Sheyna, who then invited her to join them in Denver to continue her education. "You are too young to work; you have good chances to become something," Shamai wrote. "My advice is that you should get ready and come to us. We are not rich either, but you will have good chances here to study and we will do all we can for you."

Since her parents would never permit her to go to Denver, Golda began secret preparations to run away. Sheyna and Shamai sent some money to help pay for a railway ticket. Golda borrowed some more, and earned the rest with her friend Regina by giving English lessons to immigrants for 10 cents an hour.

The night before her departure, Golda lowered a bundle of clothes out the window to Regina who carried it to the railway station. The next day, Golda would board a train instead of going to school. That night Golda felt guilty. She knew her parents would be deeply hurt, and she felt especially badly about leaving her little sister. Golda worried about what would happen to Tzipke now that both she and Sheyna were out of the house. While Tzipke slept, Golda stroked the little girl's face and kissed her goodbye. In the morning she said goodbye to Milwaukee.

Golda Mabovitch in 1915.

The accomplishments of the labor movement... were due mainly to two factors: first, these young Jews who wanted to live a life of dignity felt that they had no alternative.... Another factor was their unlimited faith in man.
—GOLDA MEIR

4

Independence in Denver

Almost as soon as she arrived, Golda started high school. She worked afternoons in Shamai's dry-cleaning shop, so that he could go on to his second job as a janitor. Golda later wrote of her years in Denver, "Life really opened up for me, although Sheyna and Shamai proved to be almost as strict as my parents and we all had to work very hard."

Golda was fascinated by the people who dropped in at her sister's home. The small apartment had become a meeting place for the Jewish immigrants from Russia who had come to Denver to be treated at the Jewish Hospital for Consumptives. Though Golda was usually the youngest person in the room, she loved listening to them talk of philosophy and social issues. It was then that Golda first became interested in the Socialist Zionists. Their political philosophy made the most sense to her. Golda was deeply moved by the idea of a national home for the Jews—a place where Jews could be free and independent and live without fear. She loved to hear about the radical intellectuals who were moving to Palestine. Golda shared their belief that if Jews worked with their own hands to build the homeland they would be earning a moral right to reclaim the land.

> *Britain is trying to prevent the growth and expansion of the Jewish community in Palestine, but it should remember that Jews were here two thousand years before the British came.*
> —GOLDA MEIR

Golda Mabovitch and Morris Meyerson shortly before their marriage in 1917.

Golda Mabovitch during World War I, when she came into contact with Americans who had volunteered to fight with Britain's Jewish Legion against the Germans and Turks. The Jewish Legion was formed in 1917, when Britain gave its Jewish immigrants who were eligible for military service a choice between enlisting or returning to Russia.

Overlooking Jerusalem, a war memorial commemorates British troops killed during the campaign of 1917-18 which liberated Palestine from the Turks. A British military administration governed Palestine from 1918 until 1922, when the League of Nations accorded Britain mandatory civil powers in Palestine, ending Ottoman Turkish supremacy.

Golda read excitedly about the work that Jews were doing to reclaim land in Palestine. To support them, she spent hours on the streets of Denver asking people for money for the Jewish National Fund. The money would be used to buy land in Palestine, even poor land—rocky, eroded hillsides, or disease-ridden marshes—from the Turkish and Arab landowners.

It was during one of the stimulating gatherings in Sheyna's home that Golda met Morris Meyerson, the brother of a young woman Sheyna had met in the sanatorium. Though he was quiet and soft-spoken, and not very handsome, Golda was attracted to him. Meyerson, as she and the others called him, knew a great deal about art and music. He was entirely self-educated and spent much of his spare time in lecture halls and in the public library. Golda admired him and was fascinated by the range of his knowledge.

Meyerson was a contemplative, gentle dreamer, who at the time barely managed to support his mother and himself on his earnings as a sign painter. Somewhat short and slight, his face was dominated by large, kind eyes which shone from behind his thick spectacles. Physically and mentally, Meyerson stood in sharp contrast to Golda, with her strong features, robust build, and determined activism.

Golda dated him and other young men in Denver, and Sheyna soon began to disapprove of her busy social schedule. Sheyna felt her younger sister should devote more time to her studies and less to running around to lectures and concerts. After about a year of bickering with her sister, Golda decided she had had enough. After all, she had not left her bossy parents to be dominated by her sister. So one night, after a particularly angry quarrel, Golda moved out to make it on her own.

Golda had to drop out of school to support herself. She spent a week with a young tubercular couple, sleeping in a little alcove in their furnished room. Because of her experience in her brother-in-law's dry-cleaning shop, she took a job in a laundry that specialized in washing lace curtains. Golda stretched wet curtains and tacked them onto wooden frames to dry. By the end of each day her fingertips were sore and bleeding, but with the first week's pay she was able to rent a small furnished room of her own.

No longer in high school, Golda took charge of her own education. Since Meyerson was widely read, she asked him to suggest books. They spent long afternoons and evenings discussing the romantic poetry of Lord Byron, William Wordsworth, John Keats, and Percy Bysshe Shelley. They went to free lectures and concerts and to the parks on Sundays. Golda began to care deeply for Morris Meyerson. She wrote to Regina of his "beautiful soul."

Finally, Golda found a job in a Denver department store where she sold dress linings and took measurements for skirts. Though she worked nine hours a day, the job was easier than stretching curtains at the laundry. However, when her par-

The Allenby Memorial monument in Jerusalem, commemorating the capture of the city by British forces under Field Marshal Sir Edmund Allenby on December 9, 1917. The regiment known as the Jewish Legion joined Allenby's expeditionary force in February 1918 and fought with distinction against the Turks and Germans in Palestine and Syria.

ents found out about the department store job they were angry. In 1914 no self-respecting Jewish girl did that kind of work. They begged her to return home and promised not to interfere with her education. Since Golda had resolved to become a teacher and since she wanted to go to school, it seemed a good idea to return to Milwaukee.

Though it meant leaving Meyerson in Denver, Golda went home to live with her parents. She studied hard and in less than two years graduated from high school and entered the Milwaukee Normal School for Teachers.

While the conversations among Sheyna's friends in Denver had been about theories and ideologies, back in Milwaukee there was more interest in action. During World War I, the Mabovitch home had become a stopping-off point for Jewish Legion volunteers. These young Jewish men had organized themselves into an exclusively Jewish unit within the British army. Their goal was to free Palestine of its Turkish rulers. Golda was deeply moved by their stories. Like them, she sought to put her idealism to use. She too wanted to fight for Palestine and was frustrated that she could not join the Jewish Legion because of her sex.

Slowly, Zionism became more and more important to Golda. She listened closely to stories about the struggle and courage of the *yishuv*, the Jewish community in Palestine. She decided that as a Jew she belonged in Palestine, helping to build the Jewish homeland.

Morris Meyerson did not share Golda's passion for Zionism. "I don't know whether to be glad or sorry that you seem to be so enthusiastic a nationalist," he wrote. "I am altogether passive in this matter." Meyerson suggested that Jews would probably suffer in one place or another, and where they suffered did not much matter to him. This difference cast a shadow over their marriage plans. Golda felt she had to persuade Morris to go with her to Palestine. In her mind, it was unthinkable that they should be separated.

In the meantime, Golda increased her political work. At meetings, lectures, and rallies in Milwau-

This generation decided that the senseless living and senseless dying of Jews must end. It was they who understood the essence of Zionism—its protest against such a debased existence. The pioneers chose to come to Palestine.

—GOLDA MEIR

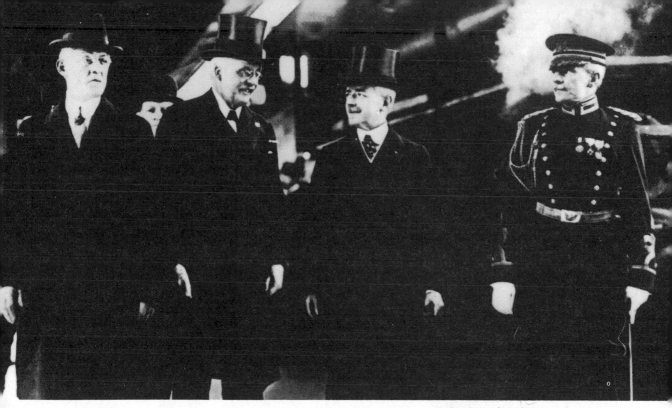

kee she was particularly influenced by members of Poale Zion, the Workers of Zion, a small, mostly Yiddish-speaking branch of the Labor Zionist movement. When they opened a *folkschule*, a part-time school at Milwaukee's Jewish Center, Golda began teaching Yiddish, a language she loved, to children a few afternoons a week. Though technically Golda was too young to join the Labor Zionist Party, local branch members were impressed by her energy and abilities and accepted her at 17.

Then, on November 2, 1917, the British government issued an official declaration (the Balfour Declaration) stating its support for the Zionist aim of restoring Palestine to the Jews. Jewish communities everywhere stirred with new hope. For Golda and millions of other Jews, the announcement meant that it was truly time to go to Palestine.

Morris Meyerson had to make a decision. He had reservations about Palestine, but he knew that if he refused to go with Golda he would lose her. So on December 24, 1917, Golda and Meyerson were married in a Milwaukee synagogue.

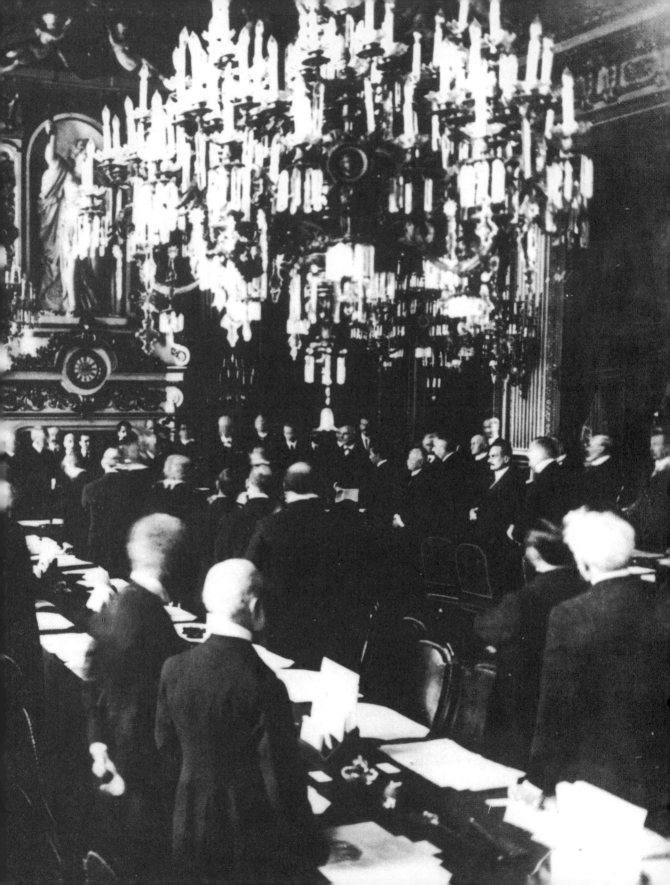

5

Living on a Kibbutz

Before leaving America, Golda chose Merhavia as the kibbutz she and Meyerson would ask to join. Kibbutz means "group" or "collective" in Hebrew. A kibbutz is a community of people who come together to work toward common goals.

The first kibbutz in Palestine had been very small. It was started by nine men and women in 1909. By 1920 this form of social organization was still in its infancy. Most kibbutzim were very strict. They had high standards, difficult goals, and tolerated little in the way of human weakness. They were working to transform "unusable" desert or marshland into productive farms, to establish a Jewish state, and in doing so, to create an ideal society.

On a kibbutz, everything—land, tools, livestock, housing, and all other goods—was owned equally by members. No one owned anything privately. For example, all clothing was kept in a storeroom and taken by members as needed. Decisions about what to buy for the kibbutz were made by the group as a whole, and all profits were turned back into building the settlement. Children were raised by all the adults. Wealth was equally distributed to all the workers of the community. Equality of the sexes was a basic principle of kibbutz life. Men and women shared equally in the work and in the benefits of their labor.

"Imagine!" Golda enthused. "Just imagine living

Golda Meyerson attends to the breeding of chickens at the Merhavia kibbutz in Palestine in 1922.

Diplomats attend the signing of the Treaty of Versailles, June 28, 1919. The treaty, which officially ended World War I, also instituted the League of Nations, the organization which in 1922 accorded Britain a mandate to govern Palestine.

by our own labor in a community where we're all equal, no rich or poor, no snobbery, no exploitation!"

Merhavia was located in the malaria-ridden Valley of Jezreel. When Golda and Morris arrived in 1921, 32 men and eight women made up the community. At first, kibbutz members were reluctant to admit a married couple, in part because they felt Merhavia could not afford the luxury of children, who required years of care before they could be productive. And some members had other objections to admitting the Meyersons. They felt that the pretty, gray-eyed Golda was a "pampered American girl" who could not endure the hard work and rough life at Merhavia. The general assembly of the kibbutz met three times before finally accepting the Meyersons.

In the autumn of 1921, Merhavia consisted of a few frame houses, a primitive shack which served as a communal kitchen and bakery, and a cluster of trees. The rest was wind, rocks, and some empty, sun-scorched fields.

When the Meyersons were invited to spend a trial period in the community, Golda worked hard to prove herself. She picked almonds in a grove near the kibbutz for days on end, and helped to plant a little forest in the rocks on the road leading to Merhavia. She learned to use a pick to hack rocks out of the ground. When she retired to her room

Students attend a philosophy class at the Hebrew University in Jerusalem during the 1920s. An internationally famous seat of learning, the Hebrew University was founded in 1918 shortly after British forces occupied Palestine.

exhausted at night, she longed to skip dinner and go right to sleep. But she did not—because the eyes of the community were upon her.

To Golda, the food at Merhavia was dreadful and boring. Chickpeas were served at almost every meal in some form, perhaps boiled or fried with onions. In addition, the community ate endless rations of canned beef and canned herring left over from the war.

So when it was her turn to work in the kitchen, Golda was delighted. At last she could do something to improve the food! She quickly reorganized the kitchen. First, she did away with the bitter cooking oil the kibbutzniks bought from the Arabs and used in almost everything. Then, she started serving oatmeal for breakfast. This idea was terribly unpopular at first. The young men and women of Merhavia claimed it was fit only for babies. But Golda explained that everyone needed a hot, nutritious breakfast before work and kept serving oatmeal until finally they began to enjoy it.

Golda's job in the kitchen brought other changes as well. Despite protests that she was trying to soften the community, she covered the tables with sheets for Friday night Sabbath suppers and decorated each table with wildflowers.

Golda's sense of the aesthetic also extended to clothing and annoyed many kibbutz members. Women at Merhavia worked in dresses that were simple sacks made of rough material in which holes were cut for the head and arms. "We tied a piece of rope around the waist, and that was that," Golda wrote in her autobiography. She didn't mind in the least that the dresses were not stylish, but she did not want to wear them wrinkled. So every night, using a heavy iron heated by coals, she pressed a "sack" and a kerchief for herself for the next day, knowing full well that some kibbutzniks might think her lacking in pioneer spirit.

In fact, for all her "American refinements," Golda *was* a true pioneer who gave everything to her work. She believed that each job she did helped to build the Jewish homeland. Of her time at Merhavia, Golda wrote, "I enjoyed everything about the kib-

Jews protesting Arab riots gather at the Wailing Wall in East Jerusalem in 1929. The site, which is part of the western wall which enclosed Jerusalem's Second Temple (destroyed by the Romans in 70 A.D.), was in Jordanian territory until the Mideast War of 1967, when Israeli forces seized control of all Jerusalem and Transjordan.

butz—whether it was working in the chicken coops, learning the mysteries of kneading dough for bread in the little shack we used as a bakery or sharing a midnight snack with the boys coming back from guard duty and staying on in the kitchen for hours to hear their stories. After a very short time I felt completely at home, as though I had never lived anywhere else."

Morris, however, found life in the kibbutz difficult and very unpleasant. The hard physical work exhausted him, and because he remained uninspired by Zionism, he derived little satisfaction from his efforts. In addition, he was a shy person, and the lack of privacy on the kibbutz appalled him. Everyone at Merhavia washed together in a communal washroom, ate together in a single dining room, and spent the after-dinner hours together in planning sessions or committee meetings. Morris longed for a more traditional domestic life with Golda. He wanted friends with whom he could talk about art and music, instead of endlessly debating every social issue.

Golda was next assigned to work in the kibbutz poultry yard. She was sent to an agricultural school for a few weeks to learn how to breed chickens. Until then, Merhavia had bought its eggs from neighboring Arabs, and considered them a great luxury. Golda threw herself into her work. Before long, poultry workers from everywhere in the valley were visiting Merhavia to learn how its chicken coops were run so efficiently.

Once they saw how hard-working and well-organized Golda was, the members of the kibbutz were quick to accept her. Within a year of her arrival, Golda was elected to the steering committee that set policy for the kibbutz. She was also chosen to represent Merhavia at a convention to discuss the future of new Jewish settlements. Since she was very articulate and fluent in English, Golda was also called on to guide important visitors through the community, and to explain its objectives.

At Merhavia, Golda demonstrated her amazing energy and talent for organizing. She perceived

Her life reads like a Hollywood script composed by an overzealous screenwriter bent on producing a spectacular on great moments in contemporary Jewish history.

—MARTIN PERETZ
in *The New Republic*

A street in Jerusalem in 1935. That year 60,000 Jewish immigrants arrived in Palestine, fleeing the growing anti-Semitism of Hitler's Germany. Palestinian Jews faced further problems in 1937, when Arab terrorism erupted throughout the country.

problems accurately and had the imagination and flexibility to provide effective ways of correcting them. She was also capable of carrying out long and complex projects, tracking each detail until it was completed. There at the kibbutz, working hard day after day, she was profoundly happy.

Though the two and a half years in Merhavia were among the most fulfilling of Golda's life, she could not ignore her husband's discomfort. Meyerson, not only unhappy, had become physically ill. The strenuous work and repeated bouts with malaria had weakened his already frail constitution. A doctor warned Golda that if her husband remained at Merhavia he would be chronically ill. In addition, the young couple wanted to start a family, but Meyerson refused to have his children brought up by other adults on the kibbutz. The couple had to reach a compromise. For her husband, Golda agreed to leave the kibbutz, find an apartment, and start a family in a more traditional setting; for his wife, Meyerson agreed that the couple would remain in Palestine.

6

Struggling in Jerusalem

In Jerusalem, Meyerson began slowly recovering, but Golda was depressed and miserable. She missed the wide open spaces of Merhavia and found city life crowded and noisy. She also felt lost without the new friends she had made on the kibbutz, and the sense of accomplishment she had gotten from her hard work. However, neither she nor her husband discussed their very different feelings about leaving Merhavia.

The Meyersons found jobs in the Jerusalem office of Solel Boneh, the Histadrut's contracting and public works enterprise. The Histadrut, or Labor Federation, was the central organization of the Jewish workers in Palestine. Golda worked as a cashier, and Meyerson became a bookkeeper. After working less than a year, Golda became pregnant and on November 23, 1924, gave birth to a son, Menachem. He was a lively, healthy baby, and both parents enjoyed caring for him.

When Menachem was four months old, Golda decided to return to Merhavia for a while. She still longed for her life on the kibbutz, and was unsure what to do about her faltering marriage. During her stay in Merhavia Golda realized she would have

A tower dating from the first century soars above a district of Jerusalem where the Supreme Moslem Council, a leading Arab nationalist organization, had its headquarters during the 1930s. Persistent Arab terrorism and agitation forced the British government to invite Zionist and Arab leaders from Palestine to a conference in London in 1939.

According to archaeologists this is the location in Jerusalem where Pontius Pilate presented Christ to the crowd which condemned him. Jerusalem has remained a sacred city to Jews, Christians, and Moslems for many years.

43

to decide which came first—her husband and child, or the kind of life she wanted for herself. After much soul-searching Golda returned to Jerusalem determined to make the best of her life as a young wife and mother.

Despite Golda's good intentions, life in Jerusalem was still very hard for her. Their two-room apartment had neither gas nor electricity. It was a constant battle to keep the dingy rooms clean. The kitchen was in a tin shack in the yard and she had only a small oil stove for cooking.

Yet, Morris Meyerson was much happier in Jerusalem than he had been in Merhavia. He loved the ancient city, its narrow winding streets and its rich, complex history. Morris felt at home and content, for Jerusalem had always been a city of poets and philosophers. On his way home from work, he enjoyed stopping to browse in the city's many bookstores.

Golda and Morris aspired to nothing more than simple nourishing food, a clean place to sleep, and a new book or record now and then. But in Jerusalem they had hardly enough money to feed little Menachem and their new baby, Sarah, who was born in 1926. Golda had suffered poverty before, but she felt bitter about having to struggle to provide enough food for her children, born in the "Promised Land."

When Menachem went to nursery school, Golda served as the school's laundress in exchange for her son's tuition. She heated each pail of wash water, then scrubbed everything by hand on a rough board. That winter was sleety and cold, but the family had no heat in their little apartment. Menachem and Sarah seemed to be sick all the time, and Golda began to despair.

Finally, Golda found work teaching English in a private school. Since she could not afford a babysitter, she brought Sarah to school with her. Though the job was easier, her life seemed an endless struggle of caring for children, cleaning house, and working to provide the barest essentials. Balancing all her obligations at once, she felt deeply frustrated, less by poverty than by the realization that she was

> *Taken as a whole, the inner struggles and despairs of a mother who goes to work have few parallels. . . . In spite of the place which her children and her family take up in her life, her nature and being demand something more; she cannot divorce herself from a larger social life. She cannot let her children narrow her horizon. And for such a woman, there is no rest.*
> —GOLDA MEIR

not living the life for which she had come to Palestine.

After four years of trying to devote herself exclusively to her family, Golda could bear no more. Though she loved her children and husband deeply, she realized that caring for them could not be her entire life. She begged Meyerson to understand. In a letter to Sheyna, she explained, "My social activities are not an accidental thing: they are an absolute necessity for me." In 1928 Golda decided to become active in the affairs of her country.

A British army camp in Palestine's Judean hills in 1936. Although the British government took military action against Arab terrorists in Palestine during the 1930s, it did not consider partitioning Palestine into separate Arab and Jewish states until 1937, when it recognized the impossibility of a reconciliation between the two peoples.

7

A New Sense of Purpose

As soon as the Labor Party heard that Golda wanted to return to work, the Histadrut asked her to become secretary of the Women's Labor Council. In this role she helped start training farms where young women learned the skills they needed to plant trees and crops in Palestine's barren soil. She also supervised the establishment of nurseries and kindergartens, which would greatly benefit working women.

In 1929 and 1930, Golda often had to travel on behalf of the Women's Labor Council. Her work brought her to the United States and twice to conferences in England. Leaving Menachem and Sarah was difficult, especially because Sarah was frequently ill. As she said goodbye to her weeping children, Golda realized that she could get used to anything, even to constant feelings of guilt.

During the first years of work after starting a family, Golda was deeply troubled by having to balance her love for her children against her political activities. In later years, public acclaim and the obvious importance of her work helped her to justify the choices she had made. But during her first years of work for the Labor Party, Golda suffered.

The road from Jerusalem to Jericho winds through the sun-scorched hills of Palestine. The British government authorized substantial road construction in Palestine during the 1920s and 1930s, aiding both commercial and military communications.

Jewish schoolchildren in Jerusalem take part in a "Jerusalem Flag" celebration in 1936. Jewish communities in Palestine placed great emphasis on education during the 1920s and 1930s, financing schools and training colleges with contributions from Zionists abroad. By the mid-1930s, 100% of Jewish youth in Palestine attended school.

Golda Meir with her son Menachem *(at right)* and French conductor Serge Baudo in 1960 after a concert given by the Israel Philharmonic Orchestra in which Menachem was cello soloist. The Israel Philharmonic gained great prominence during the 1970s, attracting famous guest conductors and continuing the Jewish cultural tradition of excellence in music.

She worried about her motives and wrestled with many doubts.

When six-year-old Sarah became critically ill with kidney disease in 1932, Golda brought her to the United States for treatment. Mcnachem, who was then eight, joined them, while Morris remained at home. The separation was to last for two years and marked the beginning-of-the-end of the Meyersons' marriage.

Working as the national secretary of Pioneer Women in America, Golda addressed thousands of women. She spoke eloquently about the society Jews were building in Palestine, a society where women and men lived and worked as equals. Her sincerity helped her to win sympathy and support for the Zionist cause. Yet Golda was unsure of her gifts as a speaker. She was always amazed by her audiences' responsiveness and the money they contributed.

By the time Golda and the children returned to Palestine, Sarah was healthy and Menachem was learning to play the cello. The children were overjoyed to see their father again.

Only a few weeks after they arrived home, Golda was asked to join the executive committee of the Histadrut. By 1936 she was in charge of all the mutual aid programs and coordinated the work policies and trade unions of various kibbutzim in Palestine. She also headed the board of directors of the Workers' Sick Fund, which provided medical care for the members of Histadrut and their families, who made up more than half of the Jewish community in Palestine.

Golda loved working in the Labor Federation, where she could put her socialist principles into action. For example, everyone in the Histadrut was paid the same basic wage, to which was added a certain amount for each dependent in the worker's family. To Golda, it was only fair that a janitor who had nine children took home far more money than she, who had only two children to support.

Though she still sometimes missed the camaraderie of life on the kibbutz, Golda felt a sense of hope and purpose in working toward the goals of Zionism.

8

Troubled Times

While Golda Meyerson was emerging as a leader in Palestine, terrible things were happening to Jews in Europe. Hitler's first attacks on Jews between 1933 and 1936 drove 70,000 to Palestine. Many of them were professionals—lawyers, doctors, teachers—and some were wealthy businessmen. They brought both skills and money to the growing Jewish community in Palestine.

The Arabs, increasingly opposed to the stronghold Jews were building in Palestine, favored Hitler and his policies, especially his persecution of Jews. On the other hand, they were alarmed to see so many Jews fleeing Europe only to settle in Palestine. They approached the British government to demand that it stop supporting the Jewish national home and refuse to allow more Jews to come to Palestine. Since 1922 the British had exercised general political control over Palestine. The Arabs also wanted more seats in the legislature and limits placed on the amount of land Jews could settle. In time the Arabs hoped they could force the British out.

Meanwhile, throughout Palestine, the Arabs attacked Jewish settlements—often burning, and looting. Though the British government sent more soldiers to protect the Jews, they had little effect.

At a conference in New York in June 1940, leading Zionist Vladimir Jabotinsky announces his intention to raise a Jewish military force to fight with the Allies. No stranger to the art of lobbying for Jewish forces, Jabotinsky had been chief recruiter for the two British regiments of the Jewish Legion during World War I.

An armed guard keeps watch at a camp housing Jewish-American settlers near Jerusalem in August 1938. British suggestions for Palestine's future had divided the 1937 Zionist Congress, where some delegates demanded all Palestine as a home for the Jews, while others were prepared to accept statehood in a small section of the country.

Jewish refugees come ashore from the S.S. *Parita,* beached at Tel Aviv in Palestine in August 1939. Beaching of vessels in darkness was an ideal way for illegal Jewish immigrants to enter Palestine undetected by the British authorities. Local Jewish communities quickly absorbed the refugees before the British discovered evidence of the landing.

The Arab hit-and-run guerrillas were swift and skilled.

In response to Arab demands, the British government finally appointed a royal commission to consider their grievances. Though it met for months, it could not reach a decision. Then in 1939, the British colonial secretary issued a white paper. The document set limits (75,000 over the next five years) on the number of Jews who could settle in Palestine until 1944. After that time, Jewish immigration could only continue with the approval of the Arabs. In addition, the white paper virtually stopped Jews from purchasing any more land. It also set a date for the establishment of a new state of Palestine in 10 years. In the new state, the number of Jews would be limited and they would live at the sufferance of the Arabs.

The entrance to the Jewish ghetto in Lublin, Poland, February 1941. As German persecution of the Jews in Europe increased during World War II, those seeking safety in Palestine faced rigidly enforced British immigration controls despite the fact that most Palestinian Jews fully supported the British in the war against Germany.

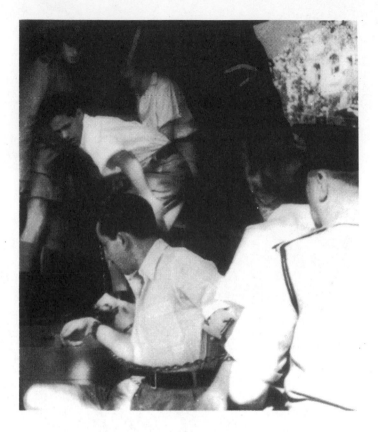

A British soldier stands guard over arrested members of Haganah, the Palestinian Jewish self-defense organization, in August 1943. Open warfare between Palestine's Jews and the British authorities had erupted in 1942 after the British victory at El Alamein in North Africa removed the immediate German threat in the Mideast.

The white paper pleased no one. The Jewish community in Palestine felt outraged and betrayed by the British. However, the Arabs were angry, too. In their eyes, the British "solution" had not gone far enough.

Jews could not stand by helplessly while Arabs attacked them. Neither could they close their eyes to the plight of their relatives in Europe. Already hundreds of thousands of Jews were dying in Nazi concentration camps. At the World Zionist Conference in Geneva, Switzerland, David Ben-Gurion said that the Jews in Palestine must fight force with force. They must arm themselves to fight Arab terrorism and to keep immigration open. Golda Meyerson agreed with Ben-Gurion, adding that as Jews, they had no alternative but to fight.

In 1940 Golda became the head of Histadrut's political department and a member of the War Economic Advisory Council, which organized resources

As the Germans retreated from eastern Europe toward the end of World War II, the victorious Soviet armies liberated many concentration camps and thus discovered the full extent of German atrocities. This official Soviet photo shows the crematorium of a concentration camp in Poland.

for the war effort and recruited Jewish soldiers. In this role she negotiated with the British on behalf of workers engaged in government works, like building roads and camps. At the same time, however, Golda was a member of the Haganah, the Jewish secret underground army. In complete defiance of British regulations, she helped to facilitate immigration and set up settlements for the newcomers.

The Haganah was literally settling Palestine by night. Teams of young volunteers would secretly carry prefabricated buildings, including huts, a watchtower, and a stockade, to an isolated spot in the countryside and put them together under cover of darkness. By sunrise, a new village stood ready for residents.

By 1941 it was clear that the differences between Golda and her husband could not be resolved, and the couple separated. The children lived with their mother in a workers' cooperative apartment house in Tel Aviv, but remained close to their father. To Meyerson's delight, Menachem, then 17, was a talented cellist and well on his way to becoming a professional musician. Sarah, on the other hand, was more like her mother, and at 14 was secretly working for a Haganah youth group.

When, after the war, the British government arrested the head of the political department of the Jewish Agency, the executive body of the Zionist movement, Golda was asked to replace him. The job was a delicate one: in effect, to lead the foreign office of a non-existent Jewish government! Though Golda worried that her training was inadequate, she agreed to do it.

At the time, thousands of Jews who had survived Nazi concentration camps were being held by the British on the island of Cyprus. The British internment camps were overcrowded and disease-ridden, and the Jewish Agency worried that children might not survive the terrible conditions. The agency won permission for families with babies to be given priority on the immigration lists so they could move to Palestine quickly. Golda took on the difficult task of appealing to people in the camps who had no children to give up their places on the

> *Golda Meir has the best qualities of a woman—intuition, insight, sensitivity, compassion—plus the best qualities of a man —strength, determination, practicality, purposefulness. So we're lucky. We have double qualities in one person.*
> —SIMCHA DINITZ
> Israeli diplomat

list to those who had.

On Cyprus, slogging through the barren, muddy camps, Golda had doubts about the work she was doing. Was it fair to ask people who had already suffered so much to sacrifice more? But despite her doubts, Golda was persuasive enough to enable thousands of infants and their parents to move safely to Palestine.

The first ship of parents and children arrived in time to celebrate the United Nations General Assembly's resolution to divide Palestine into three parts: an independent Jewish state, an independent Arab state, and an international city of Jerusalem.

A Jewish mother and her child aboard a refugee ship in 1949, en route from a British internment camp on Cyprus to a new life in Israel. Between 1948 and 1951 a half-million immigrants entered Israel, creating major social and economic problems.

9

Arming the Unborn Nation

As 1947 ended, Golda volunteered to go on another fund-raising mission to the United States. This time she sought money for weapons for the Jewish community in Palestine, because the Jews knew that as soon as statehood was declared, they would likely face an all-out war with the Arabs.

For this eventuality the Arabs were well prepared. They owned millions of dollars worth of American arms left over from World War II, and had an additional stockpile of British arms. According to some estimates, the Arabs had about 50,000 soldiers ready to fight, not including reserves. They also had artillery, armored vehicles, and an air force.

In contrast, the Jews in Palestine had almost nothing. On the day the United Nations divided Palestine, the Haganah's only fully trained striking force consisted of 3,000 soldiers. Their inventory of weapons included 10,000 rifles, 1,900 Sten guns, and 66 mortars. The Haganah had absolutely no heavy armaments, no artillery, no tanks, and no aircraft or navy. Yet, the United Nations believed that the Jews in Palestine could actually defend themselves!

Fund-raising experts predicted that Golda had taken on a nearly impossible task. They believed

A Franciscan monk worships at the altar of the Franciscan Church of All Nations in Jerusalem in April 1947. Jerusalem has long been considered a holy city by Christians, Moslems, and Jews.

British troops in Jerusalem prepare a defensive position in December 1947 in response to increasing Arab rebel activity. A few weeks earlier Golda Meyerson had entered Jordan, disguised as an Arab, to negotiate with Emir Abdullah in an attempt to keep Jordan out of the impending Arab-Israeli conflict.

The Jewish refugee ship *Exodus* in harbor at Porto Venire, Italy, in May 1947. When the British intercepted the *Exodus* at sea in July 1947, three Jews were killed and 120 wounded. When the survivors were interned in Palestine and later sent back to the British zone in occupied Germany, many nations protested.

American Jews had already depleted their funds supporting relief organizations for Hitler's victims. Nonetheless, Golda was determined to travel the country, addressing as broad a sampling of the American Jewish population as she could. She arrived in the United States in January 1948.

Golda's younger sister, who worked in America for the Council of Jewish Federations, advised her to attend their conference in Chicago. As usual, Golda spoke forthrightly and without notes. She stood before them proudly, her gray eyes searching the faces in the crowd.

"Every Jew in the country knows that within a few months a Jewish state in Palestine will be established. . . . You cannot decide whether we will fight or not. We will. . . . You can change only one thing—whether we shall be victorious. Yes, whether we fight or not, this is a decision we have to make.

American Jews protest the British government's Palestine immigration policy at a demonstration in New York in October 1945. The plight of the thousands of Jews imprisoned in British internment camps provoked increasing awareness among Zionist political leaders that the situation would not change until the British left Palestine for good.

Rescue workers survey the ruins of the King David Hotel in Jerusalem, blown up by Jewish terrorists in July 1946. The destruction of the hotel, which housed the British military headquarters in Palestine, as well as British civil government offices, greatly worsened relations between British troops and the Jewish population.

Whether we live or not, this is a decision you have to make."

At the end of her speech the crowd stood and cheered. Afterward, someone described the audience's reaction to Golda. "We had never seen anyone like her, so plain, so strong, so old-fashioned—just like a woman out of the Bible."

After two and a half months of traveling and speaking, Golda went home to Palestine with $50 million. Though she was modest about her success, almost everyone else was amazed. David Ben-Gurion said in tribute to her, "Someday when history will be written, it will be said that there was a Jewish woman who got the money which made the state [of Israel] possible."

Most of the money Golda raised was spent on arms. In one of the most daring schemes in history, and in defiance of a U.S. decision to forbid the sale of arms, Haganah teams from Palestine secretly came to the United States to purchase guns, planes, and armored vehicles to send to the Jewish community in Palestine.

Sympathetic Americans from all walks of life contributed to this underground effort. A college student transported hundreds of pounds of gunpowder

A British army unit rushes to aid a Jewish settlement in Palestine under assault by Arab guerrillas in January 1948. Following the 1947 partition proposal, that would divide the country into separate Arab and Jewish sections, Jewish settlements outside Jewish areas suffered constant attacks by Arabs.

The wreckage of a Jewish store on Jerusalem's Ben Yehuda Street, blown up by Arab terrorists on February 22, 1948. The Arab Higher Committee on Palestine had rejected a 1947 U.N. proposal for the partitioning of Palestine in a policy statement issued on February 6, 1948.

Recruits to Haganah, the Jewish defense force, undergo training in a remote area of Palestine in March 1948. Haganah preparations for the full-scale defense of the future Jewish state were far advanced by this time.

hidden inside the heavy steel body of a Cadillac. New York high school students used their skill in electronics to build a secret radio network that would link Palestine's isolated Jewish settlements and serve as a warning system in case of Arab attacks. A lawyer who had been trained by the Office of Strategic Services during World War II taught young Jews everything he knew about codes, ciphers, espionage, and commando tactics so they could do intelligence work in the coming war. Still other Americans designed guns, bought supplies, and worked out clever ways of shipping everything to Palestine.

10

Golda in Moscow

Israel's independence was to be declared on Friday, May 14, 1948 at a ceremony in the Tel Aviv Art Museum. Golda was deeply disappointed that she could not be there. She had been ordered to report to her post in Jerusalem the day before the ceremony. Reluctantly, she climbed into a little two-seater plane to make the trip.

A few minutes into the flight, the motor of the plane began to groan and rattle. Golda and the pilot became frightened. Where in Arab territory could two Jews land safely? While the pilot was searching the ground below, the drone of the engine grew worse. The pilot decided to try to return to Tel Aviv. Somehow he made it, and Golda Meyerson was present at the ceremony marking Israel's independence the next day.

Only two days after Israel had become a nation, Arab soldiers were gathering on its borders. Fighting was sure to follow. A telegram arrived for Golda from the head of the United Jewish Appeal in the United States. American Jews were celebrating the news of Israel's independence, the cable said, and now might be the time for another fund-raising tour. Although Golda wanted very much to remain in Israel during its first trial with the Arabs, she

---

Israeli aircraft mechanics remove the valuable machine guns from a downed Egyptian Spitfire fighter near El Majdal in the Negev desert in May 1948. Although Israeli forces had begun to import tanks, aircraft, and guns in large quantities from Europe immediately after independence, they also proved adept at putting captured Arab equipment to good use whenever possible.

A Haganah mortar team prepares to open fire on Arab positions in the fight for control of the Tel Aviv-Jerusalem highway in May 1948. Jerusalem was almost completely dependent on food shipments from Tel Aviv during the first six months of 1948, and fighting for control of the vital road link was especially heavy.

returned to the United States. Almost everywhere she went, she was greeted by cheering crowds and generous support for the young nation of Israel.

The first battles between Arabs and Israelis lasted about a month. Then the Security Council of the United Nations stepped in and ordered a ceasefire. During the four-week truce that followed, Israelis prepared themselves for still more action. When the war resumed, Israelis took the offensive and in 10 days of bitter fighting captured several important Arab towns, forcing the Arabs to agree to an-

Golda Meir's craggy face bore witness to the destiny of a people who had come to know too well the potentialities of man's inhumanity. Her occasionally sarcastic exterior never obscured a compassion that felt the death of every Israeli soldier as the loss of a member of her family.

—HENRY KISSINGER

other truce. Then in mid-October, fighting broke out in the south. The Israelis smashed the Egyptian line and the Arab soldiers retreated from the Negev settlements.

Just as her fund-raising trip in America neared an end, Golda received a cable from the Israeli government asking her to accept an appointment as ambassador to Moscow. She felt as though she were being condemned to exile. Now that Israel was finally a reality, would she ever again be allowed to work there?

Jews survey the damage in Jerusalem following the Arab siege of the city in May 1948. The first round of heavy fighting for the city erupted several weeks before Israel became independent. Between December 1947 and May 1948, fighting in Palestine claimed the lives of 3,000 Jews, Arabs, and Britons.

Knowing how important it was to respond to the Soviet Union's quick recognition of the state of Israel, however, Golda accepted the appointment. She returned to Israel to choose the staff for her embassy and to learn more about her duties. She was delighted when the Israeli government offered to send her daughter Sarah and Sarah's new husband, Zachariah, along with her to Russia as radio experts.

Golda and her staff arrived in Moscow in September 1948 and set up a temporary embassy in the elegant old Hotel Metropole. During their stay, the hotel flew the flag of Israel from the roof. Seeing it snapping in the cold Russian wind made Golda smile. "If only the czar could have seen that!" she said.

To keep costs down, Golda and her staff fixed their meals on hot plates in their hotel rooms. Golda ran the embassy like a kibbutz. She insisted on the equality of everyone on her staff, including the chauffeur and the cook. Everyone ate together and received the same amount of pocket money.

Hoping to meet local people, Golda made Friday night open house at the embassy. She served tea and cake to other ambassadors, visiting Jewish business executives, and members of the press. However, Russians and Russian Jews rarely came.

Members of Israel's non-combatant women's army receive instruction in grenade-throwing in June 1948. The existence of a women's auxiliary army greatly contributed to Israel's military successes in 1948, since it released many men for duty in the front line.

Golda Meir arrives at Tel Aviv airport on August 29, 1948, for her flight to Moscow, where she was to be Israel's first ambassador to the Soviet Union. Subsequent to the diplomatic exchanges of 1948, a 1949 Soviet-Israeli agreement allowed the Soviet government control of Russian Orthodox church property in Jerusalem and elsewhere in Israel.

The dining room of the Hotel Metropole in Moscow in 1937. The hotel temporarily housed the Israeli embassy in 1948.

Nonetheless, those easy, sociable evenings became a popular event in Moscow and were continued long after Golda left the embassy.

Once the first round of diplomatic introductions were completed, Golda was ready to make contact with the Jews in Russia. Though neither she nor most staff members were religious Jews, Golda asked them to go with her to the Great Synagogue in Moscow. No official announcement of their visit was made, but when the time came in the religious service for the customary blessing for the heads of state, a special prayer was said for the ambassador from Israel. Everyone in the small congregation turned to look at her.

A few weeks later on Rosh Hashanah, the Jewish New Year, the Israelis attended synagogue again. This time thousands of Russian Jews filled the street, and about 50,000 more gathered outside to pay their respects to Golda and to celebrate the establishment of the state of Israel. She listened in awe as the crowd chanted her name.

When the services were over, Golda found herself again in the crowd of weeping, cheering, laughing

Jews. She was so filled with emotion she could hardly speak. Finally, she choked out in Yiddish a single sentence, "Thank you for having remained Jews." The crowd buzzed as people passed Golda's message on to one another.

Back in their rooms at the hotel, the embassy staff sat together in emotional silence. Some cried, some sat with their heads in their hands. Each had been much affected by what he had just seen—the evidence of the daring courage of persecuted Jews.

Though Golda was thankful that her embassy was succeeding in building cordial relations between the Soviet Union and Israel, she was not happy with the life of an ambassador. The formality and restrictions of diplomacy were artificial and draining and she longed to return to the direct, hands-on hard work of building Israel.

From Moscow Golda closely followed events in Israel. After an uneasy peace settlement had been made, Israel held elections in January 1949. Soon after, Israel's first prime minister, David Ben-Gurion, asked Golda to become Israel's minister of labor. Golda was overjoyed. At last a job at home!

Golda Meir *(in circle)* is greeted by Jews in Moscow in 1948. During the late 1940s Israel's government stayed neutral in the emerging ideological conflict between the United States and Russia.

11

Building Israel

Since the new nation of Israel had never had a ministry of labor before, Golda Meyerson had to start one from scratch. It was an enormous job. Yet Golda's leadership qualities and determination enabled her to accomplish much.

One of the primary goals of the Israeli government was to make sure that every Jew who wanted to come to Israel could do so. After all, this "ingathering of exiles" was one of the main reasons for establishing the Jewish State. During Israel's first few years, the population more than doubled. Jews came from countries all over the world. In many cases their ways of life had been extremely different and adjusting to life in Israel was often difficult.

Golda took on the responsibility of supplying the new immigrants with housing and jobs. At first, most of the newcomers had to live in tent villages. To Golda the crowding and lack of human comforts were unacceptable. To correct this she ordered the building of temporary work villages. They consisted of clusters of one-room huts, made of corrugated iron, aluminum, or sometimes even canvas on wooden frames. The labor ministry's long-range goal was to build permanent concrete bungalows just outside the cities so that workers could live near their jobs.

An Arab watches Jewish settlers constructing a new village in northern Israel in February 1949. Settlement policy became the subject of heated political debate in Israel, where some people advocated unlimited expansion into former Arab areas, while others wanted to avoid unnecessary confrontation.

Israeli troops return from a raid into Jordanian territory, September 26, 1956. Between 1949, when truces concluded the first major Arab-Israeli conflict, and October 1956, when Israel launched a preventive war against Egypt, constant skirmishing took place between Israel and its neighbors.

To prepare unskilled immigrants for jobs the ministry of labor opened dozens of free vocational centers. They were staffed by experienced agricultural, factory, and health care workers. The ministry also provided money to support students in vocational schools.

Such an ambitious program suited Golda just fine. She seemed to be everywhere at once. She visited immigrant villages, inspected housing projects and roads, and talked with students learning trades at the vocational centers. Golda not only supervised the programs of the labor ministry, but she raised money in America to support them.

While another labor minister might have been more cost-conscious in evaluating projects, Golda saw everything in human terms. When cost-cutting measures in a housing project resulted in kitchens without windows, and a terribly steep step from the kitchen door to the ground outside, Golda ordered changes. She could not tolerate depriving a person who washed dishes of the simple pleasure of looking outside, or of a safe way to carry out a garbage pail.

Knowing that it was in her power to relieve even one person's suffering drove Golda on. When economists presented her with statistics indicating that the majority of Israelis were well-housed and working, Golda was not impressed. "Every unemployed man or woman is 100% unemployed," she said emphatically. "Every family that lacks decent housing is 100% miserable. Economic problems are not

Israeli infantry survey the terrain near the Egyptian town of Kusseima, October 30, 1956. Israel's aims in the short but decisive conflict were to destroy Egypt's military potential, damage the prestige of President Nasser of Egypt, and regain freedom of navigation in the Tiran Straits and along the Suez Canal.

Golda Meir, as Israel's foreign minister, meets with American politicians in November 1956 at a dinner in Boston. The politicians are *(left to right):* Senator Leverett Saltonstall, Lawrence Laskey, and Senator John F. Kennedy.

problems of numbers but problems of flesh and blood—human problems."

By 1953 Golda's ministry had trained some 30,000 immigrants for jobs. It had also implemented the construction of 52,000 temporary housing units, 82,000 small apartments in permanent concrete buildings, provided enough groceries, synagogues, and schools to serve the projects, and constructed 1,200 other public buildings!

The seven years Golda served as Israel's minister of labor were some of the most satisfying years of her life. It pleased her to see the tangible results of her work. But as Israel grew and changed, its needs changed, and in 1956 Ben-Gurion asked Golda to leave her post to become Israel's foreign minister.

12

Foreign Affairs

In early 1956 the Arab states on Israel's borders were making threatening gestures. The Egyptian government under Gamal Abdel Nasser had bought Russian-built planes, tanks, and guns and had begun training its soldiers in their use. Already, the *fedayeen*, bands of armed Arab raiders, were attacking Israeli settlements with Egypt's blessings.

Differences over how to respond to the growing Arab threat had caused a rift between Ben-Gurion and his foreign minister, Moshe Sharett. As a result Sharett resigned, and Ben-Gurion asked Golda to replace him. She accepted the challenging position, although she regretted having to leave her family and friends in Israel once again.

In July 1956 the Egyptians barred Israeli ships from the Suez Canal and the Straits of Tiran, cutting off all water traffic to Africa and Asia. Then, on October 24, Egypt announced that Jordan and Syria had joined forces with the Egyptian military in order "to tighten the death noose around Israel." In addition, the Israeli government learned that about 2,500 new fedayeen had completed their training and were ready to attack.

A few key members of the Israeli government and military met secretly and decided that Israel must

Israeli troops continue their push across the Sinai Peninsula, November 1, 1956. With the aid of powerful air support, Israeli forces advanced rapidly during the war, greatly aided by the surprising lack of opposition from the Egyptian air force.

Golda Meir prepares to explain Israel's actions to the General Assembly of the United Nations in New York, November 15, 1956. World reaction to Israel's preventive war with Egypt in 1956 was far from favorable. Even America's President Eisenhower condemned Israel's policy, which he thought aggressive.

Golda Meir is amused by a fellow delegate's remarks as she prepares to speak to the General Assembly of the United Nations, March 1, 1957. Responding to increased international criticism of Israel's policy, she announced that her government would stage a complete withdrawal of its forces from all Egyptian territory.

strike first. Golda had no doubts at all about the correctness of the decision.

A few key members of the Israeli government and military met secretly and decided that Israel must strike first. Golda had no doubts at all about the correctness of the decision, in which Israel was backed by the British and French, both angered over Nasser's nationalization of the Suez Canal.

The fighting began on October 29. In four days of fierce warfare, Israeli soldiers, driving an odd assortment of vehicles including tanks, ice cream trucks, and taxis, defeated the Egyptians. Israel overtook the Sinai Peninsula, four times the size of Israel, and the Gaza Strip, a part of Palestine occupied by Egyptian forces since 1948. Israelis also bypassed the Suez Canal and opened a sea route through the Gulf of Aqaba. On November 1 the United Nations Security Council ordered a ceasefire.

That same month, the U.N. Security Council adopted a resolution demanding that Israel withdraw unconditionally from the occupied territories. Golda was stunned that Israel could find so few friends, so little support in the United Nations. She presented her case with bitter irony:

"We are a very small people in a small barren land which we have revived with our labor and our love. The odds against us are heavy; the disparity of forces is great; we have, however, no alternative but to defend our lives and freedom and the right to security. We desire nothing more than peace, but we cannot equate peace merely with an apathetic readiness to be destroyed."

In her new role, many aspects of Golda's life changed, including her name. When Ben-Gurion asked members of his government to take Hebrew names, Golda wanted one similar to Meyerson, so she chose Meir, which means illuminate. As Israel's foreign minister Golda was determined to win allies for Israel. She also moved to a large, rather elegant house in Jerusalem, where she could receive distinguished guests. She also began extensive traveling.

In 1958 she toured the newly independent African countries of Ghana and Nigeria, and the Ivory

Golda doesn't think in terms of hours or work or "I've finished my day's work." She never closes the circle; it's always wide open. Working with her, we were all suicidal self-slave drivers.
—ZVI BAR-NIV
Golda Meir's legal adviser

Foreign Minister Golda Meir of Israel leads guests from Africa and Asia in Israel's national dance, the hora, October 17, 1959. Israel continued to increase it military preparedness at this time, cultivating a superiority in technology, training, and tactics which eight years later greatly contributed to the stunning Israeli victory in the Six-Day War.

Coast, which was about to win independence from France. Golda's warmth and energy charmed the Africans, who had never seen an ambassador quite like her. With her usual gusto, she taught a group of Ghanians to dance the hora. In return, they taught her the "high life," a complicated dance that originated on the Gold Coast.

Everywhere she traveled, Golda extended Israel's friendship and offered to share the expertise her

Golda Meir lived under pressure that we in this country would find impossible to understand. She is the strongest woman to head a government in our time and for a very long time past.
—WALTER CRONKITE

country had developed. In part, this was a political
decision for Israel clearly needed allies. However,
education is also a part of the Jewish tradition,
and for Golda, helping vulnerable young countries
typified what she said was "the drive toward social
justice, reconstruction, and rehabilitation that is
at the very heart of Labor Zionism—and Judaism."

Golda's International Cooperation Program recruited experts to work side-by-side with the peo-

Golda Meir visits a school
in Dar-Es-Salaam, capital
of the African state of Tan-
ganyika, January 1963.
During the early 1960s
Israeli foreign policy paid
special attention to devel-
oping good relations with
African and Asian coun-
tries, many of which had
recently gained indepen-
dence from European colo-
nial powers.

ple in other countries. The Israelis taught skills such as how to increase food production, how to irrigate and improve the fertility of the land, and how to fight disease.

The program was very successful. In 10 years a total of 2,582 Israeli experts had worked in Africa, the Mediterranean, Latin America, and the Caribbean. Nearly a thousand had specialized in agriculture, 354 in youth organizations, 262 in medicine and health care, 230 in education, 246 in technology, and 566 in other fields.

Though Golda enjoyed visiting many of these projects, she began to feel the strain of constant travel. "I seemed always to be either en route to somewhere or from somewhere or sick," she wrote in her autobiography. In fact, though very few people knew it, in 1963 Golda was diagnosed as having cancer of the lymphatic system. She was de-

The Knesset, Israel's parliament, in Jerusalem.

termined not to let it interfere with her work.

A year later, when she was 66, Golda Meir applied for old-age benefits under the National Insurance Law. It was a law she knew well, for as minister of labor she had introduced it. On the forms she filled out, she wrote that she was still "actively employed" and working "16 hours a day, 30 days a month." Yet, after 43 years of working for Israel, she had begun to think of retiring.

> *...any Israeli effort to stop murder and pillage, so as to make existence tolerable for its beleaguered population, is met with an outcry about the violation of peace.... The Arab states unilaterally enjoy the "rights of war;" Israel has the unilateral responsibility of keeping the peace.*
> —GOLDA MEIR

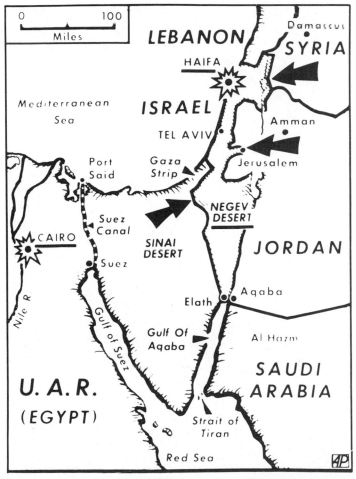

The Arab-Israeli battlefront on June 5, 1967, following the extremely successful surprise Israeli air raids on airfields throughout Egypt. Israel inflicted crushing defeats on her Arab neighbors, who had joined together, in the words of Egypt's President Nasser, to "push the Jews into the sea."

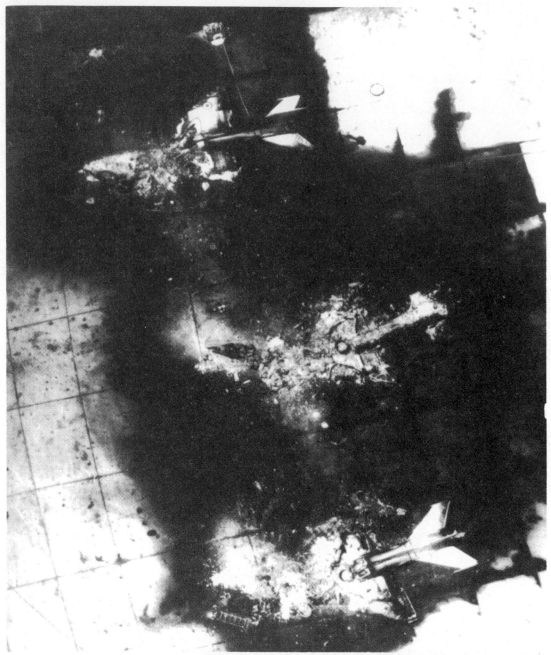

Egyptian fighter aircraft, destroyed in the Israeli air raid of June 5, 1967, lie smashed at their dispersal areas. So completely did Israel's air force surprise the enemy that few Egyptian planes got off the ground to meet the attack, and fewer still were left for operations against Israel's army.

Israeli troops in the Sinai
Peninsula take cover as
Egyptian aircraft conduct
a ground attack, June 9,
1967. Israeli army chiefs
later revealed that this was
the last Egyptian air as-
sault before Israeli troops
reached the Suez Canal.

13

The Hardest Job

Golda's desire to withdraw from public life increased, and after Prime Minister Levi Eshkol was elected, she resigned from her position as foreign minister. But her retirement was not to last. After only a few months of relative quiet, the Labor Party called on Golda to help heal a growing rift in its leadership. Believing the future of the Labor Party was at stake, Golda became the party's secretary general.

Although she had left the foreign ministry, Golda remained keenly aware of her country's precarious situation. Even as she devoted herself to furthering the political fortunes of the Labor Party, Israel's Arab neighbors continued to wage a constant war of words and deeds against the Jewish state. Every Israeli citizen recognized the terrible threat to Israel's existence.

The stage was set for renewed conflict when, on May 27, 1967, Egypt's President Nasser ordered the United Nations' peacekeeping forces to leave their positions on the border between Egypt and Israel, where they had been stationed since 1956. When the Egyptians went on to blockade the Straits of Tiran, cutting off Israel's sea access to Africa and Asia, Israel's political and military leaders knew that Egypt was preparing for war. The

Golda Meir sits alone during a parliamentary meeting in Jerusalem in August 1970, when Israeli leaders debated new American proposals for a Mideast ceasefire. After 1970 the United States greatly increased arms supplies to Israel, hoping to enhance the Israeli people's sense of security and thus create a political climate conducive to lasting peace.

Menachem Begin in 1977, shortly after he became prime minister of Israel. Begin, an ardent Zionist, favored nationalistic policies and encouraged the expansion of Jewish settlement into occupied territories inhabited by Arabs.

final signal was the massing of the Egyptian army's 100,000 men and hundreds of tanks in the Sinai.

On June 5, 1967, Israel's defence forces launched a brilliant surprise attack against Egypt by land and air. Israeli warplanes flew around Egypt in an encircling move, keeping out of radar range, and then attacked from the west—where the Egyptians least expected it. In the space of a few hours, most of the Egyptian air force was destroyed on the ground. At the same time, Israel's army attacked and captured the whole Sinai desert, taking thousands of Egyptian prisoners. Allied with Egypt by previous agreements, Jordan, Syria, and Iraq joined in the war against Israel, only to suffer as badly as the Egyptians had.

In spite of the crushing Israeli victory, Golda and many other leading Israeli politicians were afraid that any advantage gained over the Arabs could only be temporary. Their fears were confirmed when the Arab heads of state held a conference in Khartoum, the Sudanese capital, in August 1967. While deciding against any future use of force to resolve the dispute with Israel, the Arabs agreed to seek a "political solution," adding that there would be "no recognition, no negotiation, and no peace covenant with Israel." When they were informed of the new Arab policy, many Israelis, including Golda, considered it self-contradictory. They became even more convinced that the Arabs were not really interested in reaching a peaceful settlement.

When Prime Minister Eshkol died suddenly of a heart attack in 1969, the party asked her to serve as interim prime minister until regular elections were held. Golda was torn. She could see clearly how much Israel needed a strong leader, yet she honestly did not want to have to face the exhausting demands of the job. After telephoning her son Menachem and his wife, who lived with their children in Connecticut, and spending a long night in her own kitchen talking with Sarah and her husband, Golda decided to serve Israel again.

On March 7 the Labor Party's central committee voted by a huge majority to appoint Golda Meir as

Does hate for Israel and the aspiration for its destruction make one child in your country happier? Does it convert one hovel into a house? Does culture thrive on the soil of hatred?

—GOLDA MEIR
appealing to Arab delegates
at the U.N. in 1957

prime minister. Golda wept openly in response to
their vote of confidence. Honored and grateful for
their support, she still felt dazed and frightened by
the responsibilities of her new office.

Later Golda acknowledged that being prime minister was "an awful job. It's not the work," she
explained, "God knows, before I came to this office,
I was not given an opportunity to be spoiled by
leisure. I only dreamt about it. But the responsibility.
It's an awful strain."

At first Golda's doctors were worried. They advised her to rest as much as she could. Later they
had to admit that Golda's condition actually improved with long hours of hard work.

**Golda Meir attends the La-
bor Party meeting at which
the party's central committee made her premier in
succession to Mr. Levi
Eshkol, March 7, 1969. In
December 1969 Golda and
her ministers strongly opposed an American propo-
sition that Israel withdraw
completely from territo-
ries occupied in 1967.**

Prime Minister Golda Meir talks with her defense minister, Moshe Dayan, and army chief of staff Chaim Bar-Lev, at an army base in the Sinai Peninsula on April 16, 1969.

For Golda the days were never long enough. Meetings with cabinet ministers, correspondents, and foreign dignitaries were scheduled for mornings and afternoons. Golda usually averaged three speeches a week throughout the country, and regularly visited soldiers guarding the newly occupied territories.

Since daytime conferences and appointments were almost constantly interrupted, Golda held many important meetings at night around her kitchen table. From time to time she would get up to make sandwiches or chicken soup. Even in her tiny kitchen Golda was a powerful speaker, assertive about her own ideas and impatient with rambling monologues. An aide once acknowledged that arguing with her was like "arguing before a judge; when she makes a decision, it's made."

Late Saturday nights she often met with a few

key members of the Labor Party to prepare for the regular Sunday cabinet meetings. When she was accused of "baking decisions in advance" in her kitchen, Golda felt no need to defend herself. This was simply the way she did business.

To her the world was simple. Israel was surrounded by Arab enemies. Jews, while they did not always behave heroically, were her people and a force for good. Therefore people who wanted to harm Jews, either actively or through their indifference, were a negative force.

When Arabs broke the agreement to stop fighting by shelling Israeli defense forces and attacking

Golda Meir, attending the 11th Socialist International Conference in Britain, jokes with Britain's Premier Harold Wilson (at left) and Willy Brandt, leader of West Germany's Social Democratic party, June 16, 1969.

Golda Meir inspects Israeli defenses along the Suez Canal in September 1970. Israel's military leaders, who considered their positions on the eastern bank of the canal impregnable, received a terrible shock when Egyptian forces broke through the Israeli defenses in 1973.

civilian settlements, Prime Minister Meir warned, "Anybody who fails to honor the ceasefire agreement and shoots at us cannot claim immunity from the results of his aggression. Those who attack us should not be surprised if they are hit sevenfold in response." Golda lived up to her words. After each act of Arab terrorism, she ordered heavier counter-violence.

Golda Meir attends a memorial service for fallen Israeli soldiers in April 1969. The uneasy ceasefire on the Suez Canal front began to deteriorate rapidly that year, leading to frequent ground and air skirmishes. A new ceasefire negotiated by the American secretary of state, William Rogers, took effect in 1970.

Though Golda liked to pretend that she did not understand or admire military operations, the sight of a young Jewish soldier in uniform moved her deeply. To her, each one was a symbol of the dramatic reversal of the oppression of Jews that occurred in her lifetime. Golda clearly remembered a time when Jews were unable to defend themselves.

When Israeli soldiers went out on military opera-

When people ask me if I am afraid that because of Israel's need for defense the country may become militaristic, I can only answer that I don't want a fine, liberal, anticolonial, antimilitaristic, <u>dead</u> Jewish people.

—GOLDA MEIR

tions, Golda asked her aides to call her, no matter what time the soldiers got back. She often stayed up all night waiting to hear. If there were losses, Golda mourned. "We count each one," she said. "And each sorrow is not only of the mother, but of all mothers, of everybody in the country. They're everybody's sons."

Though the losses continued, Israel held firm,

Golda Meir inspects a guard of honor in October 1970 at Tel Aviv airport prior to her departure for the United States, where she was scheduled to address the United Nations. President Nasser of Egypt had died a few weeks previously and his successor, Anwar Sadat, was already considering military action against Israel.

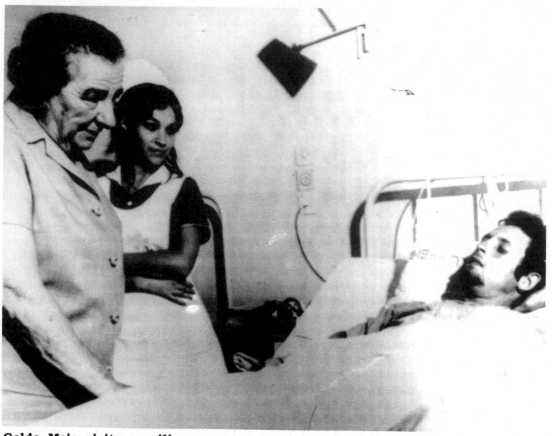

Golda Meir visits a military hospital near Tel Aviv on October 15, 1973. Although a ceasefire went into effect on the Egyptian front on October 22, Israeli forces continued to seize Egyptian territory and kept up the pressure against Syria in the north.

keeping its forces in the territories taken in the Six-Day War of 1967. While Arab guerrilla fighters stepped up their attacks, Prime Minister Meir called for direct peace talks and pressed her demands for the establishment of secure boundaries between Israel and its neighbors.

As tensions mounted in 1973, Golda's cancer spread. In April, in almost complete secrecy, she began cobalt radiation treatments. Though the after-effects of the treatments often made her sick, Golda refused to miss any of her meetings. When her aide, Lou Kaddar, was hospitalized for exhaustion, Golda used her visits to her friend as a cover-up for her own treatment sessions in the hospital.

In September 1973 Syrian troops began gathering on the Golan Heights on Israel's border. At the same time, the Egyptian army moved into place along the Suez Canal. Golda worried about the massing enemy troops, but her intelligence officers and military advisers—including Minister of Defense Moshe Dayan—insisted the Arabs were not about to attack. They advised her not to call up Israel's defense forces, suggesting that it would be considered aggressive. Their counsel proved false when fighting began on both fronts on October 6, on Yom Kippur.

"That Friday morning, I should have listened to the warnings of my own heart and ordered a callup. . . . I shall never again be the person I was before the Yom Kippur War," she wrote in her autobiography.

Eventually, with the help of American weapons and warplanes, Israel's forces pushed back the Syrians and Egyptians and penetrated deeply into their territory. But their losses were terrible. More than 2,500 Israelis were killed.

In the aftermath of the 1973 Arab-Israeli War, Golda Meir visits troops on the Syrian front.

Golda Meir and senior officers visit Israeli forces on the west bank of the Suez Canal on October 29, 1973.

A storm of protests followed. Were the terrible casualties necessary? At first Defense Minister Dayan's judgment was questioned. Later, the protests ballooned until Golda Meir's entire government was under attack. Prime Minister Meir listened, but she did not believe the majority of Israelis agreed with the protests.

Criticism swelled within the government as well. Golda became hurt and angry listening to the opposition party's leaders denounce her. Chief among them was Menachem Begin. She was determined not to be forced from power. However, when members of her own Labor Party began to criticize her defense minister, Golda became discouraged. Putting together a new government that satisfied all the factions in the party seemed impossible. So, on April 10, 1974, Golda Meir resigned. "I have come to the end of the road," she said. "It is beyond my strength to continue carrying the burden."

Prime Minister Golda Meir receives a salute from a
police officer as she leaves the Israeli parliament
after tendering her resignation on April 11, 1974.

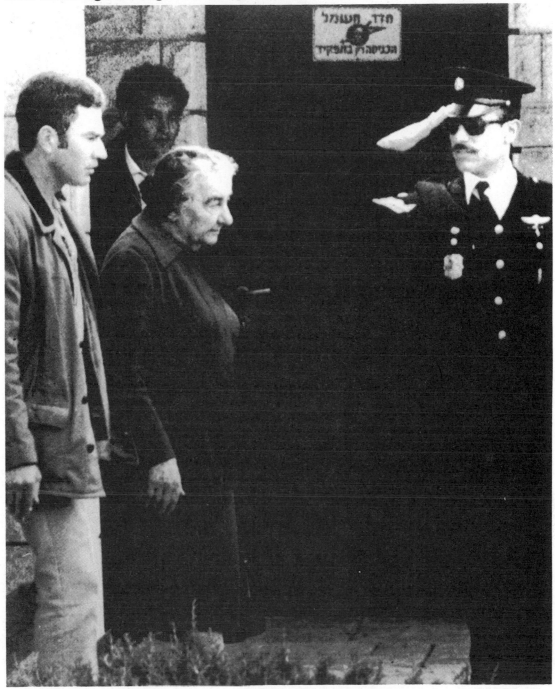

14

The Last Years

After her resignation Golda did not have time for the relaxing, quiet life she had hoped for. Instead, members of the Labor Party called on her daily for advice. Golda's phone rang so often that she had her already unlisted phone number changed four times!

Golda continued to remain interested in the political life of the country, but the changes she saw saddened her. She was especially disheartened when voters rejected the Labor Party in 1977. Her old enemy, Menachem Begin, became prime minister.

Egyptian President Anwar Sadat's decision to discuss peace with the new Begin government in Jerusalem was especially bitter for Golda. After all, she had tried to make contact with him. Though she stood in the receiving line to greet Sadat at the airport, it was hard to accept the limited role of an honored guest.

Golda found it harder still to watch the progress of the Arab-Israeli peace talks from the sidelines. When critics accused her of having missed opportunities to make peace as early as 1971, she was deeply hurt. Haunted by these criticisms, Golda became determined to set the record straight. Though she was often ill and her energy level was declining, she would face her critics and present the facts.

Golda started preparing for a press conference in

> *Golda Meir was a noble foe who always proved that she was a political leader of the first category, worthy of occupying her place in your history and worthy of the place she occupied in your leadership.*
> —ANWAR SADAT
> president of Egypt

Internationally famous actress Ingrid Bergman as Golda Meir in an American television documentary filmed in Israel in 1981.

Golda Meir confers with President Anwar Sadat of Egypt in Jerusalem on November 21, 1977. Sadat's peace-seeking visit to Israel greatly improved Western opinion of the Arab states and paved the way for further negotiations in September 1978.

Israeli troops carry Golda's coffin at the funeral ceremony, December 12, 1978.

which she would defend herself. She rallied her friends and former aides to begin gathering documents and organizing material. However, some information was hard to track down and the Begin government seemed slow in granting approval for the document search. Nevertheless, Golda persisted, despite her almost constant pain and frequent stays in the hospital. The idea of correcting the public's opinion of her leadership was important to her.

On October 19, 1978, Golda entered Hadassah Hospital in Jerusalem for the last time. Though she was still making plans for the press conference, her strength was clearly ebbing. At 80 years of age, and after fighting cancer for 15 years, Golda was dying. She wanted only her family and closest friends by her side.

Rain was falling on Tuesday, December 12, as a crowd of hundreds gathered in the cemetery. The mourners, among them Golda's friends and family, and leaders from around the world, listened to the drone of the ancient Hebrew burial prayers rise above the patter of the rain.

The funeral was as Golda wanted it—simple and without eulogies. Yet, at the grave, and in countries all over the world, mourners silently praised this remarkable woman's strength, vision, and life-long dedication to building a Jewish nation.

Chronology

1898	Born Golda Mabovitch in Kiev, Russia
1906	Moves to Milwaukee, Wisconsin
1909	Forms the American Young Sisters Society
1912	Runs away from home to live with her sister in Denver, Colorado
1914	Returns to Milwaukee and becomes active in the Labor Zionist movement
1917	Marries Morris Meyerson
1921	Moves to Merhavia, a kibbutz in Palestine
1924	Moves to Jerusalem and has her first child, Menachem
1928	Becomes secretary of the Jewish Federation of Labor in Palestine
1932	Returns to America to serve as the national secretary of Pioneer Women in the United States
1934	Joins the executive committee of Histadrut
1936	Directs the Workers' Sick Fund in Palestine
1940	Becomes head of the political department of Histadrut
1941	Marriage ends in a separation
1946	Becomes the head of the Jewish Agency's political department
1947	Travels to the United States and raises $50 million for arms for Israel
1948	Appointed Israel's ambassador to the Soviet Union
1949-56	Serves as Israel's minister of labor
1956	Last name hebraized to Meir
1956-66	Serves as Israel's foreign minister
1966	Serves as secretary general of the Mapai Party
1969	Becomes prime minister of Israel
1977	Meets with Egypt's President Anwar Sadat
1978	Dies after 15-year battle against cancer

Further Reading

Davidson, Margaret, ed. *The Golda Meir Story.* New York: Scribner, 1976.

Gibson, William. *Golda.* New York: Atheneum, 1978.

Mann, Peggy. *Golda: The Life of Israel's Prime Minister.* New York: Washington Square Press, 1973.

Meir, Golda. *My Life.* New York: Putnam, 1975.

Slater, Robert. *Golda: The Uncrowned Queen of Israel.* New York: Jonathan David, 1981.

Syrkin, Marie, ed. *Golda Meir Speaks Out.* London: Weidenfeld & Nicolson, 1973.

Index

Karen McAuley, a graduate of Bennington College, has written several textbooks and devised educational programs for high school students. She resides in New York City.

Arthur M. Schlesinger, jr. taught history at Harvard for many years and is currently Albert Schweitzer Professor of the Humanities at City University of New York. He is the author of numerous highly praised works in American history and has twice been awarded the Pulitzer Prize. He served in the White House as special assistant to Presidents Kennedy and Johnson.